D0374927

SELLING
OUT

Also by Joey Green

Hellbent on Insanity
(*with Bruce Handy and Alan Corcoran*)

The Unofficial Gilligan's Island Handbook

The Get Smart Handbook

The Partridge Family Album

Polish Your Furniture with Panty Hose

Hi Bob!

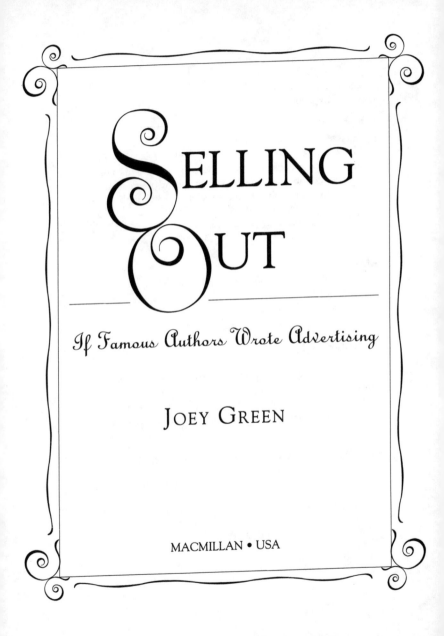

SELLING OUT

If Famous Authors Wrote Advertising

JOEY GREEN

MACMILLAN • USA

Special Thanks to:
Natalie Chapman, Traci Cothran, John Vasile, and John Fiore Pucci.

MACMILLAN
A Simon & Schuster Macmillan Company
1633 Broadway
New York, NY 10019

Library of Congress Cataloging-in-Publication Data available

ISBN: 0-02-860843-7

Manufactured in the United States of America

10 9 8 7 6 5 4 3 2 1

For Debbie

Contents

CONTENTS

CONTENTS

CONTENTS

Introduction

When Mark Twain described a classic as "a book which people praise but don't read," he did so in the pages of *Puddin'head Wilson*, an unopened literary classic. So it should come as no surprise that recent surveys reveal four out of five Americans think Oscar Wilde makes hot dogs, H. P. Lovecraft manufactures fiberglass boats, and Anton Chekhov is a character on *Star Trek*.

But let's face it, if any one of us made a concentrated effort to read every book ever written, we wouldn't even get past *Books in Print*. Sure, Fyodor Dostoyevsky was a literary genius, but who's got the time to read 240 pages into one of his books just to find out what the crime is, let alone the punishment? After all, if brevity really is the soul of wit, Shakespeare would have done us all a favor and written *Hamlet* as a sonnet.

INTRODUCTION

So what is literature? In short, literature consists of those books summarized in *Cliff's Notes*, assigned as required reading in college English classes, labeled satanic by suppressive, ignorant religious fundamentalists, and sitting unread on your bookshelf. Let's just say it's lots of interesting words strung together and dotted with punctuation marks and arranged into sentences until they add up to stories. It's similes and symbols, it's foreshadowing and Formica, it's analogies and aftershave, it's metaphors and Methodists. It's man versus nature, butter versus margarine, synthetics versus cotton washables. Yes, it all boils down to one part fiction, two teaspoons of narrative, a pinch of motif, and a squeeze of imagery—all sauteed in allegory, delicately seasoned with symbolism, and garnished with doggerel.

But what if American authors courageously compromised their integrity to pursue more accessible themes in their works? Wouldn't convenient bite-size chunks on commercial topics (and perhaps sponsored by large corporations) better help Americans harness their horizons? Or would that lack poetic license? Well, mine doesn't expire for at least another year, so let's just see how an array of authors might better sell out.

Catcher in the American Express

In the style of J. D. Salinger

Do you know me? You probably wouldn't know me from a hole in the wall. In fact, I'm sure of it. I don't mean to say that I don't have any outstanding features or anything. I just don't think we've ever met, that's all. The funny thing is, the only people who ever end up recognizing you are the ones you can't stand. That always kills me. I swear to God, it drives me crazy. I'm not kidding. It annoys the hell out of me if you really want to know the truth.

Anyway, the really important people never know who you are. Like the waiters in bars for instance. It's the goddamn truth. So when I go into a bar I put on an act like I'm a regular there. I'll tell the waiter to bring me the usual. When the guy gives me the once-over, I'll act really surprised. I'll tell him I drink Scotch and soda like he forgot or something. I'll say it smooth as hell too, because if you trip over yourself the waiter can tell you're pulling his leg because you're underage, and then he won't serve you. The waiters I know are usually pretty sharp, but when they ask me for some ID, I give them an icy stare like I've been terribly insulted. I'll start acting like a hotshot, like I own the place or something. "You oughta know me by now. Caulfield. Holden Caulfield." I put on this very mature voice so they won't suspect my age for a minute.

"Certainly, Mr. Caulfield," says the waiter. He's lying through his teeth so I won't feel insulted or anything. That kills me. I've never been to this place in my life, and the waiter starts acting like he's known me for years. He just doesn't want me to walk out, that's all. I can usually get a lousy drink with that line, but the only trouble is, sometimes you run into a real stickler. He'll be very nice and polite about it so you don't get all steamed up, even though he's really knifing you in the back.

That's when I pull out my American Express card. I don't say a word, I just let the card speak for itself. It impresses the hell out of people, it really does. They fall for it every time. They think you're some kind of big shot just because you've got this crummy plastic card with your goddamn name on it. All of a sudden the waiter's bringing me drinks and I'm really putting it away. People start waiting on you hand and foot, they really do. You feel like goddamn royalty. I'm not kidding.

You can feed them every line in the book sometimes and they won't budge an inch. But just pull out that old American Express card and you're somebody special. Whenever I'm in a really tight spot, it works like a goddamn charm. I really mean it. American Express. Don't leave home without it for Chrissake.

Please Don't Squeeze the Charmin

In the style of Bernard Malamud

Leon Whipple bit his knuckle and looked down the aisle of the cold grocery store. He was the store manager, fatigued, steely dry, with a balding head of hair graying at the sides, a bristling mustache, and round glasses. He was sixty, in a clean white grocery apron, and haunted by trouble. He stood alone, helpless, staring at a display he had stocked earlier that morning, waiting for the inevitable. He shut his eyes to escape the terror, but the image was stuck in his mind, a darkness filled with shoppers pushing their silver carts past the towering pyramid at the end of the aisle, unaware of Leon's plight, their faces shadowed by the fluorescent lamps, their hands clutching for packages of the paper good, as Leon's arms flailed in helpless protest.

He felt for his back pocket, lifted his glasses from his thin face, and touched his hollow eyes with the hand-kerchief. The pain and woe made him to the bone weary, and he prayed to God for help. "Why will this torment not stop?" he despaired. And Leon wept.

The pain was maddening. How many times had he fruitlessly pleaded his case to the women? Why should they not listen? It seemed to Leon such a small request. Day after day he waited for them, living in agony, questioning the necessity of it. Perhaps if he warned them that if they so much as got near the display he would throw them out into the street. He had often considered the idea but he could not bring himself to do such a thing. Oy, to live in such a condition. He felt defeat daily; he could not communicate with these women, could not understand why he could not awaken their hearts to his simple needs. He felt a terrible anguish.

A cart pulled up to the display, and two women appeared from behind it. Leon shuddered, but he stood still, peering, his heart growing heavy with suspicion. The first woman reached out and took a package from the shelf. She was telling her friend about the tissue, the package now cupped in her hands; she glanced behind her nervously, undecided whether to do anything more, but the temptation was too great. Leon waved his arms in rage.

"Ladies, ladies!" he shouted, his face lit up with affliction. "Please don't squeeze the Charmin!"

The two shoppers glanced nervously at each other.

"But it's irresistibly soft," the first woman answered.

This angered him. His gestures were impatient. I must put an end to this, he thought. But his words did no good, for the moment he turned his back on them, they were at it once again. He begged, pleaded, whimpered for the women to let him live in peace; he could take misery no more.

"Here try it," the second woman said, putting a package of tissues into his pale hands. This made him dizzy.

"My God!" he cried to himself, distress showing in his eyes. He denied the softness he felt, resisting it on principle, but the touch was smooth in his hands. He felt a momentary joy and then the eyes of the women were upon him.

"Mr. Whipple!" they exclaimed.

The Golden Arches

In the style of William Carlos Williams

two all beef patties
special sauce

lettuce cheese pickles
onions

on a sesame seed
bun

Where's the Beef?

In the style of Friedrich Nietzsche

Before one attempts to pinpoint the exact location of the beef, one must first acknowledge that this location will only be temporary since the beef is not likely to remain in the same location forever. Hence, the actual discovery of the beef's location in its totality is meaningless and will provide no real satisfaction in the realm of the human experience. The discovery itself eventually runs into nothingness; only the act of discovery gives meaning. The existence of the quest makes for a truly human history. Without it, only despair is left. Thus, by discovering the true location of the beef, humankind only succeeds in bringing about its own downfall. It is, after all, far more important to know the essence of the beef than to

discover its location in any single point in time. Therefore the location of the beef is of no relevance; only the
search for its essence gives humankind authenticity.
Where then is the beef? The beef is dead.

I Can See Myself in the Dishes

In the style of Nathaniel Hawthorne

There was once a time when the newly wed Sylvia Melbourne had taken it upon herself, as is custom, to invite her mother-in-law to a turkey supper. Before proceeding further, I will merely hint that Sylvia Melbourne felt a deep anxiety toward the meeting on account of a certain impression which she desperately desired to affect upon the mother of her husband. As is not infrequently the case with women unfamiliar with the affairs of matrimony, Sylvia worried herself into a quandary over the possibility that something might go awry. It was therefore with extreme solicitude that she settled the preparations for the feast. It is a circumstance worth mentioning that the precious china with which Sylvia set the table was cleansed with a peculiar potion; and it was this mysterious formula that lent the tableware great luminosity.

The occasion was rendered more interesting after Mrs. Melbourne, the mother of Sylvia's husband, arrived at their homestead, and when all three had taken their seats at the supper table. The effervescent glitter emanating from the place settings drew the notice of Mrs. Melbourne. Looking deeply into the plate before her, she could discern the figure of a face returning her glance, strangely reflecting an almost maiden splendor of irresistible charm. The serving piece seemed to possess magical properties, and her eyes grew clear and bright.

"I can see myself in the dishes!" exclaimed an amazed Mrs. Melbourne, raising the plate before her. She looked into the ceramic platter, invigorated by the youthful reflection that answered back. How Mrs. Melbourne then lavished her daughter-in-law with praise! Yes! Sylvia was the worthiest of those deserving admiration!

In truth, Sylvia had rinsed the china with Joy, no ordinary dishwashing liquid. The magic powers, however, did not lie in the realm of the mystical, but rather in the potion's strong cleansing properties, which enabled one to see one's reflection in the dishes. For those preoccupied with their own image shall always see more in their reflection than what nature provides, and like Mrs. Melbourne, their egotism is easily harnessed.

Reach Out and Touch Someone

In the style of Gertrude Stein

Someone from home called to share a smile today. A smile from someone reaching out to touch someone out of touch. A happy voice to make you feel that wherever you go, you're not very far from wherever you go to reach out and touch someone calling to share a smile. Long distance is the next best thing to being wherever you go to reach out to touch someone not very far from home calling to share a smile. Someone from home reached out to touch a happy voice to make you feel that you're not very far from the next best thing to being there . . . Click. Buzz.

Deposit eighty-five cents for the next three minutes please.

A phone is a phone is a phone.

Alka-Seltzer

In the style of Kurt Vonnegut

It is late evening. A violent storm is going on. It feels like the end of the world. The storm is in my stomach. My name is Kilgore Trout. I am a science fiction writer. I live in a small apartment in the basement of the Chrysler building in New York City. My stomach is upset. Plop plop, fizz fizz.

I went to a lavish party this evening. It was a buffet dinner. I do not mean to say they served buffet. You would think a buffet is some type of bird. It is not. A buffet is a smorgasbord. There were stuffed cabbages, egg rolls, cold cuts, and Swedish meatballs. Each Swedish meatball was skewered with a toothpick decorated with a tiny Swedish flag. I do not know why they are called Swedish meatballs. I asked one of the waiters if he knew. He told me the meatballs are imported from Sweden. I did not believe him. I filled my plate with them anyway. Plop plop, fizz fizz.

A waitress sauntered over to where I was standing. She held out a platter filled with little squares of cheese stabbed with tiny plastic swords. I filled my plate with them so I would be properly armed in case the party broke into a miniature sword fight. I plucked one of the flags from my Swedish meatball. Armed with one of those flags and a little plastic sword, I felt ready to invade Grenada. Plop plop, fizz fizz.

The fact is this: I felt as though I could eat a horse. I would never actually eat anything wearing a saddle. My wife, Magnolia Trout, told me I ate like a pig. I have never seen a pig eat. I asked Magnolia if pigs use silverware. She did not answer. "Touché!" I said, brandishing one of my little plastic swords. Plop plop, fizz fizz.

I have never understood why there are so many expressions for animals. For instance, you can be sly as a fox. You can be quick like a rabbit. You can be slow as a snail. Right now I feel sick as a dog. Plop plop, fizz fizz.

A battle is raging in my stomach. I am stuck in time. What I mean by that is: I cannot suddenly jump ahead ten years to the planet Tralfamadore where my stomach is no longer gurgling and gargling. Plop plop, fizz fizz.

Now I see why Swedes export their meatballs.

Rosie's Diner

In the style of Ernest Hemingway

The door of Rosie's Diner opened and Nick Adams came in. He sat down at the counter. He had entered the diner and was now sitting on a stool.

"What'll it be?" Rosie asked. She wanted to know if Nick wanted something.

"Coffee," said Nick.

"Anything else?" asked Rosie.

"No, that will be all," said Nick.

"You're sure about that?" asked Rosie. She wanted to make certain Nick had a chance to reconsider.

"Yes," said Nick. "Just coffee, thank you."

Rosie brought Nick a cup of coffee. It was in a heavy white mug.

"Cream or sugar with that?" asked Rosie.

Nick shook his head no. He liked his coffee black. Nick brought the mug to his lips. It felt warm in his hands. He sipped the coffee slowly. When Nick finished, he set the mug down on the counter.

"Refills on that?" asked Rosie. She wanted to know whether Nick wanted more coffee.

Nick thought for a moment. He considered the idea. He mulled it over. Yes, he would go for another cup. Nick nodded his head. He picked up the coffee mug for Rosie to refill it.

Rosie moved to pour more coffee into the cup. But Nick was not holding the mug under the pot's spout. The coffee poured from the pot. But it missed Nick's cup. Coffee spilled out over the counter.

Nick had not meant for this to happen. He stood up and stepped back from the counter. He reached into his back pocket and took out his handkerchief. He was going to sop up the puddle of coffee from the counter.

"Put that away," said Rosie. She held a roll of paper towels in her hand.

Nick studied her curiously. He was looking her over.

"Nothing to worry about," Rosie insisted. "It's Bounty, the quicker-picker-upper."

"I don't know," said Nick. He was not altogether certain that the paper towel could absorb the coffee better than his handkerchief.

"Watch," Rosie said. "I'll take a piece of Bounty in one hand and a piece of the leading two-ply brand in the other." Rosie laid them both down at the same time over the coffee spill. Nick watched the two paper towels soak up the coffee. The leading two-ply brand was fast. It was very quick. But it was nowhere near as fast as the Bounty.

Nick was quiet. He did not say a word. He had nothing to say. Otherwise, Nick might have said something. Rosie looked up at him. "You're probably wondering whether it's strong enough," she said.

21

Nick had not considered this. He only wanted another cup of coffee. He remained silent. Rosie turned on the sink faucet. Cold water poured from the spigot. Rosie stretched out a piece of Bounty with her two hands. She held it taut. She ran it under the water. The Bounty got wet. The paper towel was damp now. It was soaking. Rosie held it out in front of Nick.

"Now take your mug," said Rosie. "Put it right on top."

Nick hesitated. He did not know what Rosie had in mind. He picked up his mug and placed it on the wet paper towel that she held out in front of him. He did not think it would support the weight of the heavy mug. But the Bounty did not tear. It held up under the weight. Rosie bounced the mug up and down on the paper towel, and it still did not rip.

"It really is strong," admitted Nick. "I guess it's Bounty for me." He was going along with her. He was not interested in seeing any more demonstrations.

"Now how about that coffee?" asked Rosie.

Nick nodded. He thought she would never ask. This time, Nick had no intention of letting it spill. He had seen enough for one day.

Own a Piece of the Rock

In the style of Arthur Miller

Willy Loman, the salesman, depressed and hurried, rushes out the front door of his home. From offstage we hear a car door open and slam shut. The motor starts, and the music rises in intensity as the car pulls out from the driveway.

BIFF LOMAN, *rushing out the front door in fright:* Pop! No, wait! Pop!

The music crashes down in a frenzy of sound. Biff stands in the doorway, looking out into the street. Panic rushes his senses. He turns around slowly, closes the door, and moves back through the living room toward the telephone sitting on a corner table. In a state of shock, he picks up the receiver and slowly dials a seven-digit number, concentrating on each number.

BIFF, *nervously, into the receiver:* Hello? Prudential? *He stands there, holding the receiver. A quiet sob rises in his throat. Then, relief:* You mean, I'm covered!?!

Music fades up as the lights cut to black.

Ring Around the Collar

In the style of Albert Camus

I was with my wife when a woman standing behind us complimented me on my shirt. I suppose I should have been flattered by her uninvited praise, I can't really be certain. She continued to admire my choice in clothing when her face suddenly expressed severe dismay. She then told me, with great emotion, that I had a ring around my collar. I suppose I should have been thankful for her telling me; so I thanked her very much, and then she gave me a long look which made me feel rather uncomfortable. I realized I should not have thanked her. I suppose I should have been taken aback, I can't be sure.

My wife launders my clothing, and she seemed somewhat distraught. I told her it was quite all right;

it really did not matter to me anyway since I could always buy another shirt. This did not seem to comfort her, but I really didn't see any reason why this ring was of such importance. To be frank, I did not particularly like this ring, but it did not particularly trouble me either. I did wish this woman hadn't made such an issue of it. I must say I didn't much relish her company. I had the impression she thought I was in great sorrow over the situation at hand, but in point of fact, I was hardly concerned. After all, there are others in the world with dirt stains much worse than my own. I simply shrugged my shoulders to gesture indifference. She gave me a queer look; she seemed to have misinterpreted my gesture as resignation, and this, naturally enough, provoked her further.

"Those dirty rings," she spoke out, which rather startled me. "You try washing them out, you try scrubbing them out, but you still come out with ring around the collar."

I was thinking how strange it was that this woman was insisting on this. I was ready to tell her to leave me in peace when she addressed me gravely, and her tone became urgent. She seemed to me like a religious fanatic, preaching "Cleanliness is next to godliness"; I felt as though I had to cleanse myself of a ring of dirt in order to be absolved of some cardinal sin. While pondering this, I missed what she said; the only things that really caught my attention were isolated phrases and gestures. What she was aiming at, I gathered, was to charge that my wife had laundered my shirt wrongly. She pointed her finger at me and made me feel that my wife had no alternative but to use a specific laundry detergent. It seemed to me that this woman's speech showed a certain frankness, and everything she said sounded quite feasible. I really didn't think the matter deserved such urgent attention to begin with, but I didn't feel like speaking up and getting into a lengthy discourse. Anyway, it hardly mattered; I was destined to live this fate, and this woman's arguments seemed rather pointless. I had a ring around my collar, yes, but at least I had that, and it made little difference in the scheme of things if I did anything about it.

i wish i were an oscar mayer wiener

In the style of e. e. cummings

oh, i wish
i were
        an oscar mayer wiener
that is what i truly
want to be

because if i were (an oscar mayer
wiener) everyone would be in love
            with me

oh, i'm glad:i'm not an oscar
        mayer wiener—
that is
what i'd never   want to be

SELLING OUT

because if

i were
(an oscar mayer
wiener),
there would soon be nothing
               left of me

Tidy Bowl

In the style of Herman Melville

Call me crazy. It was not the sight of a great white whale off the starboard side of the *Pequod*, the resultant pounding of fierce waves and their subsequent dizzying foam, or another one of Captain Ahab's frenzied, raving tirades, but rather the mixing of the excessive lard in that morning's breakfast with my gastric juices that compelled me to rapidly descend the gangway from the deck to the cabins below to find the ship's head. After exorcising the demons dancing in my belly—lo!—the toilet failed to flush.

It is one of the more curious facets of a large sailing ship's anatomy that the toilet tank is perhaps the most complex contraption on the vessel. The device itself is monstrous in design, but, it is only by understanding the marvels of the flushing mechanism that you can truly come close to comprehending the immediacy and complexity of my precarious circumstance. As for my precise knowledge of the intricacies of the internal workings of the toilet tank, I am indebted to my distinguished shipmates, Starbuck, Queequeg, and Mr. Stubb, who, among their many other talents, professed a remarkable ability to wield a plunger as keenly as they could hurl a harpoon.

To any one not fully acquainted with the inner workings of a toilet tank, the task of repairing the fixture might seem absurdly hopeless. The flush handle on the outside of the toilet tank turns a trip lever, essentially nothing more than a long metal stick, inside the tank. When the handle is turned downward, the trip lever inside the tank rises, pulling a lift wire which raises the tank ball that covers the outlet valve. Essentially, a twist of the handle pulls the cork from the rum bottle—although in this case the cork itself is hinged to the bottle; hence, the water inside the toilet tank empties through the outlet valve, filling the toilet bowl. As the water empties from the tank, a float ball bobbing on the water's surface, looking something like a rubber bladder, descends inside the tank. A thin rod attached to the plunging float ball opens the ball cock—a spring-activated faucet that allows more water to fill the toilet tank—lifting the float ball back up again until the tank is filled and the ball cock is shut off.

Though like most men I had only a vague notion of how to fix this apparatus, and while I cared not to carry out any repair beyond my abilities, I was compelled to remove the lid from the toilet tank. Imagine my consternation, my sheer astonishment, my unbridled incredulity at discovering inside the toilet tank, floating on the surface of the water, a queer little man sitting in a white dinghy and strumming a ukulele. To be frank, I was convinced this was an apparition brought on by my aforementioned bout with virulent dyspepsia, particularly since the gentleman looked like a miniature version of Ahab himself, peg leg and all.

"Captain Ahab?" said I.

"Ahoy! Methinks killing everything that lives in these waters is the only course of action to be taken," soliloquized the little man. "Vengeance is mine! All the foul sea creatures, from the accursed bacteria to that sinister white whale, shall answer to my wrath! 'Twas they that brought this wretched stump upon me! With every flush these waters be disinfected now! Chemicals are me harpoons. The calculating malice of these brutal creatures must be purged from the waters! They mock me; they beckon me; they outrage me. The scourge and disease these inscrutable creatures foist upon mankind must be eradicated! Their very existence is madness, a pure evil, that by reason must be obliterated! We must see to it that every toilet bowl is a tidy bowl! Are ye with me, mate? Are ye? Speak, ye blathering boil on the buttocks of humanity! Avast!"

Impulsively, I reached for the toilet handle and flushed. Just as I had outlined earlier, the flush handle hoisted the trip lever, pulling a lift wire, raising the tank ball that covered the outlet valve. The cork was pulled from the rum bottle; the water inside the toilet tank started emptying down the outlet valve; the small boat began spinning, caught in a microcosmic maelstrom, until the concentric circles of the whirlpool engulfed the tiny lifeboat, its maddened peg-legged passenger, and a petite ukulele, sucking them round and round the vortex and finally down through the outlet valve.

I must confess that to this day I do not know for certain whether the tidy bowl man was a hallucination or a genuine human being. But this much I will admit: I was not looking forward to lunch.

Shout It Out

In the style of William Shakespeare

SCENE I. A ROOM IN MACBETH'S CASTLE.

*Enter Lady Macbeth with a basket of dirty laundry,
Lady Macduff, and Macduff.*

LADY MACBETH: Out, out, damned spot! out, I say!
Mustard on a green shirt, lo! Ketchup on a blue
shirt, hark! Grass stains, blood stains! What! will
these garments ne'er be clean? I pre-wash!
I pre-soak! Here is the stain still! All the stain
removers in the kingdom will not clean these
blots from my life. What's splotched cannot be
unsplotched. A dry cleaner! A dry cleaner! My
kingdom for a dry cleaner!

LADY MACDUFF: My lady, this stain, have you tried to Shout it out?

LADY MACBETH: That is exactly what I am doing! Out, damned spot! Out, I shout! Out! Out! Out!

MACDUFF: That is all she does. It is a compulsion with her, to shout at soiled clothing. I have known her to do so for several hours. Some say she's mad.

LADY MACDUFF: Behold, Lady Macbeth; when I say Shout it out, I refer not to the use of words, but a stain remover whose name is Shout.

LADY MACBETH: You mean, I have been shouting at clothing for no reason! Hast thou not made a fool of me? Doth not the entire kingdom think me a raving lunatic! Out! Out! Out!

[Exit Lady Macbeth.]

MACDUFF: Unnatural troubles breed more stains than natural fabrics. Her mind is blemished, not her garments. More needs she the divine than a stain remover.

[A cry of a woman is heard.]

LADY MACDUFF: What was that shout?

Enter a Messenger.

MESSENGER: The queen, my lord, is dead.

[Flourish. Exeunt.]

Put a Tic Tac in Your Mouth and Get a Bang Out of Life

In the style of Carlos Castaneda

It had been fifteen years since I had seen don Juan, but it seemed as if no time had passed as I watched him finish eating his tuna melt. We were sitting at a booth in a Ramada Inn on the outskirts of Guadalajara, Mexico. I picked up the check. Next to the register stood a rack filled with an assortment of chewing gum and candies. I reached for a box of Tic Tacs and told the cashier to add them to the check.

I held up the small clear plastic box and shook it. The little white candy pellets rattled like beans inside a maraca. "Breath mint?" I offered don Juan, snapping open the plastic white lid.

Don Juan laughed.

This made me self-conscious.

I wasn't sure whether he was mocking me. "Why are you laughing?" I asked.

His face became serious. "You see, but you do not *see*," he said.

Something in his voice aroused a feeling of trepidation in me. There was an uncomfortable silence between us. I sensed that don Juan felt I was not comprehending a deeper meaning. "Does this breath mint mean something?" I asked, breaking the silence.

"It's not simply a breath mint," replied don Juan suddenly. "It's the clean, fresh explosion of mint."

I considered this for a moment, but I could not organize my thoughts coherently. "I don't follow you," I said.

Don Juan took a Tic Tac from the box and held it between his thumb and index finger. "You must open your mind to the possibilities," he said. "It is a matter of perception. The reality of this dimension is inhibiting your ability to glimpse the fleeting world." With that, don Juan placed the white candy between my lips. I felt no apprehension and took it inside my mouth, letting it roll on my tongue. A tingling sensation enveloped me immediately. I felt fireworks exploding in my mouth. Don Juan held my shoulders. I tried to smile but I was overpowered by the urge to giggle.

"Focus!" ordered don Juan, jolting my shoulders.

Suddenly I became aware of don Juan's face.

PUT A TIC TAC IN YOUR MOUTH AND
GET A BANG OUT OF LIFE

He was staring me in the eyes, and yet, I only saw a luminous glowing white orb, radiating, pulsating with rhythmic movement, like a giant Tic Tac with strands of light emanating from all sides. Looking around, the whole room was fibrous, like an iridescent cobweb, connected, yet interdependent. For an instant, the fizzling in my mouth had propelled me into a separate reality, where I remained suspended and enveloped in a profound haze of cosmic proportions, which dissipated just as quickly. I found myself standing next to don Juan in the lobby of a Ramada Inn.

I told don Juan in great detail what I had seen. He was completely uninterested. "You are dwelling on the experience, rather than its meaning," he said. "What did you *see*?"

"You tell me," I insisted.

Don Juan laughed. "You are always insisting on having me tell you what you have seen. How can I tell you what you have seen when I have not seen what you have seen?"

"I *see*," I said, although I still did not understand what he was talking about.

Don Juan seemed to be scrutinizing me. "I put a Tic Tac in your mouth," he said in a severe tone.

I reflected on this. The bewilderment I experienced was overpowering. I felt completely disoriented and confused. I could not piece together any logical conclusion, and my mind suddenly went blank. I was at a loss for words. "Yes, but what happened?" I asked.

Don Juan peered at me. He was exasperated. "You got a bang out of life!" he exclaimed.

I was puzzled. "How can I know that for certain?" I asked.

Don Juan looked deep into my eyes. He remained silent for a long time, then looked to his feet. "I don't know how to say this," said don Juan, putting his arms on my shoulders. "I think you may have a learning disability."

Let Your Fingers Do the Walking

In the style of Robert Frost

Two fingers walk across a yellow page—
They meander past names and numbers,
Seeking a repairman whom to engage,
They stop by a list of plumbers.

I dread going out in the deep white snow,
Walking twelve long miles into town
Hoping to find a plumber who will know
How to fix frozen pipes before sundown.

I opened the phone book with a sigh,
And searched through the thick gazetteer.
Two fingers crossed a yellow page, since I—
Know if it's out there, it's in here.

SELLING OUT

I tell you this, there's no use talking,
I know this will sound like nonsense—
I let my fingers do the walking
And that has made all the difference.

The Coca-Cola Manifesto

In the style of Karl Marx

The history of all society is the history of thirst. Bourgeoisie and proletariat, capitalist and communist, socialist and anarchist, hoi polloi and plebeian, misanthrope and miscreant, in short, all have thirsted for a better life.

Thirst has played a revolutionary role in history. It is, after all, a base need that manifests itself in naked self-interest if left unsatiated. The proletariat is compelled to make do with the crudest tap water while the bourgeoisie imports bottles of overpriced mineral spring water across the continent, sometimes across great oceans. This inequity creates an irreparable rift in society. The ruling class, its extravagant thirst quelled, becomes an insulated and callous oppressor;

the working class, left to thirst for something greater, becomes an oppressed class.

There is, however, a soft drink refreshing the world, a great equalizer that can correct this gross imbalance. Let us consider the value of Coca-Cola in reckoning the hostility between these two opposing classes.

First and foremost, Coca-Cola is the pause that refreshes. It not only satisfies, but an icy-cold bottle of Coca-Cola is coveted by the aristocrat, the bricklayer, the gourmet chef, the street cleaner, the impoverished doctor of philosophy expelled from Prussia, anyone with a thirst crying out to be quenched. Indeed, Coke is it— the greatest taste you'll ever find.

Moreover, in the revolutionary movement against the existing social order, Coke is the real thing. Class distinctions are dislodged by Coca-Cola. That is to say, a prince cannot buy a better bottle of Coca-Cola than a peasant. The quality of Coca-Cola is not only uniform, but it in itself forces even the most obstinate aristocrat to capitulate to a pleasure enjoyed by the masses. By imbibing Coca-Cola, the bourgeoisie and proletariat come to recognize, on a visceral level, that political equality is an attainable utopian ideal and begin to thirst instead for the realization of this balanced society. Accordingly, to call Coca-Cola the opiate of the masses would be heresy. It is precisely this contact with Coca-

Cola that is needed to bridge the antagonism between the classes. But as every class struggle is a political struggle, the distribution of Coca-Cola thus becomes a revolutionary movement to overthrow bourgeois supremacy and seize political control by the proletariat. To this end, Coke adds life.

In this sense, things go better with Coca-Cola. The abolition of private property goes better with Coke; state control of the means of production goes better with Coke; a dictatorship of the proletariat goes better with Coke; centralization of the banks in the hands of the state goes better with Coke; state control of the press and transportation goes better with Coke; the inevitable class struggle to overthrow capitalist oppression goes better with Coke. In a word, life is much more fun when you're refreshed. Ultimately, I'd like to buy the world a Coke.

Workers of the world, have a Coke and a smile!

The Maidenform Woman

In the style of Jane Austen

Elizabeth Bennet was quite taken with Mr Darcy although Darcy himself had not taken notice of her. It was generally assumed by the ladies of Longbourn that Darcy was a disagreeable, horrid man filled with arrogance and conceit, fancying himself God's gift to the world. So high and mighty was he, they thought, that he had little time for anyone else, let alone any need for a wife. Darcy lived alone in Pemberley, and just the fact that he had once attended a ball and failed to muster the bravado to ask any of the women to dance with him filled the ladies of Longbourn with disdain for what they considered his shocking rudeness. Catherine considered Darcy a lout after he neglected to say "You're welcome" after she said "Thank you" to him for holding a door open for her; Lydia referred to him as ill-mannered for failing to offer her his handkerchief when she feigned a sneeze to prompt his chivalry; Jane playfully called him a vile man with unrestrained pride for offering to fill glasses at the punchbowl for Miss Bingley and Lady Charlotte, but not for herself; Mary was heard to whisper under her breath that Mr Darcy was a savage philistine for stepping on the foot she had placed in his path, even though he apologized profusely before continuing on his way across the room.

As for Elizabeth, she too believed that Darcy had a repugnant disposition and she found it impossible to believe that he could ever be civil and gentlemanly after exhibiting such barbaric behavior. Yet, Lizzy found herself helplessly attracted to the man with the rugged physique and animal magnetism precisely because of his frightful traits that would undoubtedly inhibit him from lifting his pinkie finger while drinking a cup of tea, knowing which fork to use at dinner, or stifling a yawn in the presence of company. Elizabeth wondered how she could even consider social intercourse with this pariah, let alone entertain the idea of connubial bliss; he was a feisty and indecent man; but she also imagined that he was equally feisty and indecent in more conjugal pursuits; more importantly, she wondered how would she ever get Darcy to take notice of her womanly largess.

Mrs Bennet, hazarding that her daughter Lizzy harboured an ardent fondness for Mr Darcy, coaxed her husband to invite Darcy over to Longbourn for tea one Tuesday afternoon under the pretense of discussing a fanciful business proposition. "If we are ever to get Lizzy a husband, we must show Mr Darcy every cordiality," Mrs Bennet told her daughters gathered in the vestibule. "I dare say, Lizzy, if you are to succeed in luring Darcy to return your affections, you had better show some ingenuity."

While Mr Bennet and Mr Darcy sat in the drawing-room, the women of Longbourn, in fashionable long dresses and petticoats, entered the room with all the preparations for afternoon tea. Catherine passed out the Royal Doulton tea cups; Lydia poured the Earl Grey tea from the matching teapot; Jane wheeled in a pastry cart full of scones with clotted cream and jam; Mary passed out linen napkins embroidered with the family crest. Elizabeth, wearing a full-length winter coat and feeling it incumbent upon herself to kindle Mr Darcy's ardor, gathering all her fortitude, put herself before Darcy, unfastened the silver buttons on her overcoat, and let the garment fall from her shoulders to the floor. A strange hush fell over the assembled. Elizabeth was wearing only a lacy brassiere and panties.

Mr Darcy was eyeing her with unrestrained awe; his mouth and lips were dry; his heart beat rapidly. It vexed him to see Elizabeth exposed in only her undergarments, yet his eyes could not help but caress her delicate curves. "Good Lord," cried Darcy with an air of gallantry. "You are a vision of loveliness!"

"The Maidenform Woman," said Lizzy, blushing with felicity. "You never know where she'll turn up."

Rabbit Keeps Going and Going

In the style of John Updike

Running in his bright blue jogging suit, Harry "Rabbit" Angstrom, the long-forgotten high school basketball champion of yesteryear, unconsciously beats the big marching drum he carries in front of his middle-aged paunch. Passing the Rinalto theater, he remembers when he first dragged Janice and Nelson to see *2001* when they lived in Penn Villas, right before Janice ran off with Charlie Stavros and Skeeter came and a girl named Jill died when Harry's house burned down. In *2010* they reactivate HAL, Rabbit recalls, reminding himself of the five pages on personal computers in *Consumer Reports*, still debating in his mind the merits of a Power PC, not quite sure how many megabytes of RAM he really needs. Extra

memory would allow Rabbit to run more complex pro-
grams, and these days Harry figures he can use all the
memory he can get, since his own seems to be fading.
Age. You can't run away from old father time. Although
now you can capture it with the right VCR. Last month's
issue spent four pages rating ten different brands. With
a video camera you can even record your own home
movies. The kicks Webb Murket could get with a VCR.
As for Harry, he'd videotape the Weather Channel so he
could watch the forecast at his own convenience. Rabbit would rather be back home now, sitting in his La-Z-
Boy lounger watching HBO, although this month he has
already seen *Yentl* three times. He regrets having to miss
tonight's television lineup: "Wheel of Fortune" at seven-
thirty, "Mad About You" at eight, "Hope & Gloria" at
eight-thirty, "Seinfeld" at nine, "Friends" at nine-thirty,
and "ER" at ten. Although television really hasn't been
the same since Sonny and Cher broke up. The beat goes
on, he muses, pounding his drum.

Rabbit wonders whether he made the right decision
running out on Janice for the umpteenth time, taking
nothing with him but this ridiculous marching drum,
leaving his son Nelson in charge of Springer Motors,
wondering if he'll come back only to find the entire lot
of Toyotas reduced to a virtual scrap heap, picturing
dented steel, shattered windshields, stripped urethane

bumpers, mangled headlights dangling from their hollow sockets by color-coded wires, that ungrateful son of his behind the wheel of a Tercel, shifting back and forth between drive and reverse, his foot pressed to the floor, slamming recklessly into every car on the lot as if they were nothing more than bumper cars. As a kid Harry loved the bumper cars, remembers one Saturday riding them for hours and hours with his sister Mim until he finally gave in and agreed to take her on the Round-Up with its dizzying red cars that circled and spun and looped and whipped and twisted them around for what seemed like an eternity, stopping just in time for Rabbit to heave a day's worth of corn dogs, popcorn, and cotton candy out behind the roller coaster. Funny how life is always being compared to a ride on the roller coaster. It's a lot more like a ride on the Round-Up. Terrifying.

Rabbit loves running to the beat of a different drummer, remembers when life seemed to stretch out ahead of him, before Janice told him she was pregnant with Nelson, and Harry was suddenly switched onto a side track like an abandoned box car, reminding Harry of the way his father could never get Rabbit's Lionel locomotive to stay on the tracks on Christmas morning under the tree when they lived on Jackson Street. In Monopoly, owning all four railroads means collecting two hundred dollars each time a player lands on one. Rabbit sees himself as the little metal boot, running defiantly past Indiana Avenue, Illinois Avenue, B. & O. Railroad, Atlantic Avenue, Ventnor Avenue, and Water Works to land hopelessly on Marvin Gardens with its poisonous red hotel bringing the rent up to twelve hundred dollars. He never lands on Free Parking. Never gets to pick up the five hundred dollars in the middle. A trip to the drugstore could have saved him the anguish. If only they'd taught that in school instead of making him memorize the elements on the periodic table: hydrogen, helium, lithium, beryllium, boron, carbon, nitrogen, oxygen, fluorine, neon, sodium, magnesium, aluminum, silicon, phosphorous, sulfur, chlorine, argon, potassium, calcium, scandium, titanium, vanadium, chromium, manganese, iron, cobalt, nickel, copper, zinc, . . . the names pound through Rabbit's skull. Harry could never understand why so much useless information was drummed into his head; he can still recite the name of every U.S. president: Washington, Adams, Jefferson, Madison, Monroe, Adams, Jackson, Van Buren, Harrison, Tyler, Polk, Taylor, Fillmore, Pierce, Buchanan, Lincoln, Johnson, Grant, Hayes, Garfield, Arthur, Cleveland, Harrison, Cleveland, McKinley, Roosevelt, Taft, Wilson, Harding, Coolidge, Hoover, Roosevelt, Truman, Eisenhower, Kennedy, Johnson, Nixon, Ford, Carter, Reagan, Bush, Clinton. Talk about Trivial Pursuits.

Running across Brewster, still beating the drum, Harry notices a young woman of about twenty-five sitting alone on a bus bench. The long cinnamon hair cascading off her shoulders ignites a wild hope in him, makes his heart race. Harry cannot discern whether she is the quiet girl who years before came into his showroom. He itches to discover whether she has his blue eyes and Ruth's fragile pale features, yearns to speak with his illegitimate daughter, still finds perverse exhilaration in the possibility, but fights the impulse to speak to her now. Rabbit turns quickly and stumbles; he scrambles, still banging his drum, fear filling the space between beats. Running. Always running; he runs; ah, Rabbit runs. He runs like long-lasting Energizer batteries. He keeps going and going.

The Avon Lady

In the style of Emily Dickinson

The doorbell rings loudly—
Surprised, I hold my breath—
Who would ever visit me—
I fear it must be Death.

I dare not move at all—
Right here is where I stay—
If I sit perfectly still—
Death might just go away.

The doorbell rings again—
Death will not let me be—
Surmising I am home,
Death knocks persistently.

"Who's there?" I softly ask—
The words stick in my throat—
"Avon calling," comes a voice—
Heavenward I float.

One Flew over the Cuckoo for Cocoa Puffs

In the style of Ken Kesey

As an Indian back on the reservation I sometimes wore feathers just like the bright orange feathers on cocky Cuckoo Bird. The Acutes are all sitting in chairs in the day room, facing Nurse Ratched. Cuckoo Bird is trying to pull people out of the fog.

"Why can't we have Cocoa Puffs for breakfast?" he asks. "I can't speak for the rest of the boys, but I for one am sick and tired of eating corn flakes every single goddamned day. What I'm asking for is a little diversity, Nurse Ratched. I'd like something other than corn flakes. I think the boys here would enjoy Cocoa Puffs."

"Mr. Cuckoo Bird, the purpose of this meeting is group therapy, not the ward's breakfast menu selection."

"I'm just saying Cocoa Puffs at breakfast might do these birds a world of good. Variety is the spice of life for Christsakes."

"We can't simply change ward policy to suit your personal tastes. The breakfast menu has been carefully planned to achieve a delicate balance that would be thrown into upheaval by even the slightest readjustment in the routine."

"Screw the friggin' routine," says Cuckoo Bird. "This is a democracy, ain't it? We can change the damn routine. All you birds who want Cocoa Puffs at breakfast raise your hands."

"Give us Cocoa Puffs, why dontcha?" says Cheswick, raising his hand. Out of the corner of my eye I see other hands coming out of the fog. "I'd l-l-l-like to tr-tr-tr-try Co-co-co-cocoa P-p-p-p-puffs," stutters Billy, raising his hand. Martini's hand goes up too, then Spivey's fingers reach for the sky. Harding raises his hand too.

"That's only twelve votes," says Nurse Ratched.

"What's that supposed to mean?" asks Cuckoo Bird.

"There are twenty-four patients in this ward. You need a majority to change ward policy."

"What kind of chicken shit is that? Those other guys are comatose."

"This meeting is now adjourned," says Nurse Ratched.

Cuckoo Bird steps over to where I'm holding a broom. "Come on, Chief," he says. "You'd like Cocoa Puffs for breakfast, wouldn't you? A little change would do you good. Raise your hand, Chief. Come on, big fella, put them fingers high in the air." The fog is clearing and I think about having something for breakfast other than those stale corn flakes and I slowly raise my hand.

"Lookee here, Nurse Ratched. The Chief's raised his hand! That's thirteen votes. What do you say to that? Huh? We've got a majority!"

"The meeting was adjourned, Mr. Cuckoo Bird. You're only making a spectacle of yourself."

"You castrating bitch," yells Cuckoo Bird. He lunges for her, grabs her by the throat, and wrestles her to the floor, squeezing with all his might, his fingers tightened around her neck. Nurse Ratched gasps for her life until the three black boys in their white shirts and black bow ties pry Cuckoo Bird's fingers loose, drag him kicking and screaming down the hallway, strap him to a padded table, and shackle his wrists and ankles.

The doctor forces a rubber-hosed tongue protector in his mouth, coats his temples with graphite salve, and places a thin pair of silver headphones over the spots. He cranks a few dials, flips the heavy black switch, and sends the volts through Cuckoo Bird's head.

Cuckoo Bird's back arcs underneath him, his body jerks spasmodically, his breathing becomes fierce, and they give him a few more jolts, until he is wheeled out of the Shock room on a gurney, defiantly squawking, "I'm cuckoo for Cocoa Puffs! Cuckoo for Cocoa Puffs!"

Dr. Pepper and Mr. Hyde

In the style of Robert Louis Stevenson

Edward Hyde's head pounded violently. He opened his eyes slowly to find himself lying on the floor of a dark laboratory, a queer grime covering his clothing. His breathing lapsed into hideous, spasmodic grunting. He snarled. Sluggishly, he rose to his feet, his mind a cesspool of swirling images, the thought of a cool, refreshing beverage beckoning him with an irrepressible sense of urgency.

The ugly little man's lecherous eyes combed the laboratory with fiendish truculence. On the table, a beaker filled with a brown, bubbling mixture threw off a strange, sweet aroma. Edward Hyde snorted fiercely. Face hot and sweaty, stubble darkening, hair in disarray, he reached for the beaker filled with carbonated liquid, held the effervescent concoction to his lips, and drank ravenously in one gulp. The piquant prune soda seized him immediately; surely this preparation was the most original soft drink ever in the whole wide world.

Mr. Hyde tensed suddenly and flung the bottle to the floor, clutching the table, pulling the array of beakers and test tubes to the floor. His eyes bulged. He felt terrifying pangs and a spiritual metamorphosis of unimaginable proportions. Fire pumped through his veins. He gurgled rabidly, tossing his head from side to side, and the next moment, Mr. Hyde let out a long, howling, exalted scream. His face began to melt, his features grew diffuse, swelling, regenerating, contorting, undulating madly. He cackled maniacally.

Mr. Hyde shook his head violently as if to clear it. Then, suddenly, he felt himself again; the maddening pains subsided abruptly. "Arrgghhh," he announced to himself, delighting in the stupor which had overcome him. A perverse euphoria possessed him. He felt animated, volcanic, headstrong. An irrepressible revelry streamed through his head. The frothy beverage threw a spell of jubilant inebriation over him, filled him with demonic exhilaration. The combination lock to the safety deposit box of the evil Edward Hyde's soul had been cracked, and an exalted Dr. Henry Pepper had emerged from his disposition, grinning ecstatically, a spritely glint in his eyes.

Dr. Henry Pepper laughed hysterically, wiped the beads of sweat from his forehead with a sweep of his arm. He fixed his shirt-sleeves, fastened the buttons on his cuffs, adjusted his collar properly, and tucked his shirt-tail into his trousers. He let out an exultant cry. He could feel the blood coursing through his body. An ecstatic sensation seized him, and Dr. Henry Pepper suddenly burst into song. "I'm a Pepper, he's a Pepper, you're a Pepper, she's a Pepper!" he sang, dancing across the laboratory floor. "Wouldn't you like to be a Pepper, too?"

Charlie Tuna

In the style of F. Scott Fitzgerald

In retrospect I cannot honestly say whether the advice my father gave me as a susceptible youth resulted in my propensity for procuring intimate confidences from mere acquaintances without the least provocation. Quite possibly I may simply possess an innate magnetism that compels eccentrics to reveal their riotous secrets to me. In any case, upon joining a new school of fish I no longer desired to be encumbered by this questionable gift, although Charlie Tuna, with his brash yearning for acceptance by the pretentious upper crust for which I held such strong disdain, proved to be an exception.

Charlie was possessed with the idea that only his lack of good taste impeded his admittance into the most affluent circles, so he preoccupied himself with acquiring objects of impeccable taste to elevate his social standing. From the wreckage of the sunken *Titanic* he acquired an original Manet and an original Monet. He mused that his dining room table was surrounded by a Louis the Fourteenth chair, a Louis the Fifteenth chair, and a Louis the Sixteenth chair found in the remains of a French galleon. He drove a gorgeous Rolls-Royce that had been shipped overseas in its own private cabin on the *Andrea Doria*.

But Charlie was not simply obsessed with procuring extravagant objects. He also spent all his waking moments trying desperately to acquire culture. He hired a private tutor to learn to speak fluent Portuguese. He took violin lessons. He was born Catholic but, upon learning that Catholics were seldom admitted to certain country clubs or made the trustees of certain corporations, announced to the world that he was Presbyterian.

And then there were the parties. In the sweet summer nights orchestrated music spilled from his home, pierced by saxophones, oboes, and trombones. By high tide his guests were dancing like darting angel fish, the laughter bubbling, reckless chitchat ebbing from the glimmering throng in waves, the cocktails floating round. Upstairs in the arch of a balcony stood Charlie in a white flannel suit, bright blue silk shirt, a striped yellow tie, and horn-rimmed glasses staring up to the black star-kissed sky beyond the sea, possessed by the green light flashing just above the ocean surface. The distant green light flickered from a yacht owned by Daisy Starkist. I learned from Charlie that he had acquired all this culture so that Daisy would take notice of him.

"What's your opinion of me now, old sport?" Charlie suddenly asked.

I was at a loss for words.

"I'll tell you the truth, old sport," confided Charlie. "I came into this world just outside of Martha's Vineyard. I was educated among the finest schools. I inherited a great deal of money when my father was swallowed by a whale." His voice quivered when he said that, but I was convinced it was all a fish story. Charlie had ingeniously fabricated a life story replete with summers in the Mediterranean, military service in the Adriatic Sea, and business dealings in the Caribbean.

"You can't buy your way into someone's heart," I ventured.

"Of course you can, old sport." Charlie proceeded to explain how the Daisy Starkist Company selected tuna fish with only the best taste and how he had accumulated objets d'art and attained erudition so he might be chosen to be among the lucky few close to Daisy Starkist.

The idea staggered me. Charlie was convinced that Starkist only sought tuna with the finest taste, when in truth, the canning company wanted only the best-tasting tuna. Charlie Tuna failed to grasp this because he was blinded by his breathless love for Daisy Starkist. I had never before encountered any fish who desired to be fished from the sea by the Starkist Company. Surely Charlie Tuna's zeal for acceptance into a stratum far above his own was nothing more than a thinly veiled death wish.

"I have good taste, old sport. I have a wine cellar filled with Dom Perignon, I have a china cabinet filled with Waterford crystal, and shirts . . . have you seen my shirts?" Charlie opened a mahogany bureau and pulled out silk shirts and striped shirts and plaid shirts and polka dot shirts of maroon and beige and vermillion. "Look at these shirts!" he yelled up toward the ocean surface. "I have good taste! I have the finest taste!"

A fishing hook on a line suddenly dropped down next to Charlie. A note hung on the hook.

"Sorry, Charlie," it read. "Only the best-tasting tuna get to be Starkist."

O Fab! I'm Glad!

In the style of Walt Whitman

O Fab! I'm Glad! I'm ecstatic! I'm thrilled!
When I clean the laundry, my soul feels fulfilled!
A cup of detergent, a twist of a knob,
The washer fills with water, it makes my heart throb!
　　O fine washables! O permanent press!
　　　　A washing machine is the machine I love best!

O Fab! I'm Glad! when the rinse cycle begins!
It hums and it gyrates, it whirls and it spins!
O what a marvel of ingenuity!
The rinse cycle fills me with rapture and glee!
　　O wash and wear! O whiter whites!
　　　　I love a machine that gives me brighter brights!

SELLING OUT

O Fab! I'm Glad! when the spin cycle starts,
The clothes spin briskly, the water departs.
When the washer stops, and I sense no more rotation,
I open the lid, overwhelmed with exhilaration!
　　O delicate knits! O clothes that look like new!
　　　　O Fab! I'm Glad! They put new lemon-freshened
　　　　　　borax in you!

A Tale of Two Deodorants

In the style of Charles Dickens

It was the best of smells, it was the worst of smells, it was the age of fragrance, it was the age of stench, it was the epoch of good hygiene, it was the epoch of wretched body odors, it was the season of Cleanliness, it was the season of Perspiration, it was the spring of freshness, it was the summer of vile pungency, we had washed and showered, we were sweating profusely, we were dry and refreshed, we were moist and dank, it was Sure under the left arm, it was the leading deodorant under the right arm—in other words, the comparison was being made between two deodorants, both having been applied simultaneously under opposing arms, and whichever underarm proved driest by day's end would determine which was the superlative product.

It had originally been suggested that the king and queen on the throne of England command all their loyal subjects to use Sure deodorant; the king and queen on the throne of France would then order all their citizens to use the leading deodorant. A non-partisan commission of Lords and Ladies would be carefully chosen to travel to both countries and determine which deodorant was more favourable in keeping the populace dry and fresh, but this plan was abandoned after it was noted that the French peasantry bathed with less frequency than their English counterparts.

There was little contest posed by encouraging the populace to determine the efficacy of the new deodorant by using Sure under the left arm and the leading deodorant under the right arm. It was likely enough that since the overwhelming majority of humanity was right-handed, the right underarm would produce more perspiration than the left, and it was also likely to presume that since the masses were instructed to use Sure under their left arm, they were sure to deem it winner of the comparison test. Thus were the scores of gullible creatures—the creatures certain that Sure kept them drier—urged to "Raise your hand if you're Sure." Yet, despite this charade, I know this to be true. It is a far, far better deodorant than I have ever used.

Fly the Friendly Skies

In the style of Erica Jong

I have been in search of the absolutely pure, illusionary, and elusive zipless fuck all my life, but the closest I have ever come to realizing that unattainable fantasy was aboard a United Airlines flight from New York to San Francisco that I nearly missed had it not been delayed five minutes leaving LaGuardia. I was initiated into the Mile High Club by the pilot in the rest room while flying over the Rocky Mountains that John Denver is always singing so highly about. Actually it was me who did the initiating. I was sitting in my seat reading either *The Story of O, Lady Chatterley's Lover,* or *One Day in the Life of Ivan Denisovich* when the pilot, looking like Cary Grant with a cleft chin, devilish blue eyes, and a dapper blue uniform to match, but somewhat languid like William Holden in *Sunset Boulevard*, came waltzing down the aisle, determined to milk the cobra. Like a giddy schoolgirl, I unbuckled my seat belt and followed after him, slipping into the cramped rest room compartment before he could close the door. I pulled the sweater my grandmother had knit for me over my head, wondering what would happen if Christ chose this exact time and place to announce the Second Coming while my pilot and I were gearing up for our first. I un-zipped my pilot and we made beautiful turbulence to-gether. It was a hypnotic, passionate, platonic, uniquely anonymous, terse Sperm-a-thon. There was no talk at all, no ulterior motives, no guilt, no shame, no two-drink minimum, no gratuity, no dealer prep option, just pure, unadulterated, rockets' red glare, five-star zipless-fuck magic as together we flew United. Wordlessly, we emerged from the compartment—me returning to my seat, my pilot love toy vanishing into the aptly named cockpit. When the plane landed in San Francisco and I was getting off with the other passengers, about to pass the steward-esses mechanically waving bye . . . bye . . . bye . . . my handsome pilot appeared from the cockpit and pinned a pair of plastic wings to my sweater above my heart with a knowing grin, consummating, if you will, our zipless fuck, which is why, to this day, whenever I fly anywhere, I make it a point to fly the friendly skies of United.

Portrait of the Leprechaun as a Young Man

In the style of James Joyce

—Catch that Leprechaun! yells Stephen Icarus.

He runs, hair tousled, toward an elf sitting on a log in the woods eating a bowl of cereal with a spoon.

—He's got frosted Lucky Charms!

—Gadzooks! cries the little man wearing all green.

He grabs his box of Lucky Charms cereal and leaps over the log and races into the woods never stopping to look behind him self-consciously aware that his narrow escape and flight through the woods might very well symbolize the long-running suppression of the Irish at the hands of the English or perhaps the tediously long history of the Roman Catholic church if not the agelessness of Irish folklore or the twelve labors of Hercules.

—Always after me Lucky Charms. They're magically delicious. Yellow stars. Pink hearts. Green clovers. Blue diamonds. Red balloons. Purple horseshoes. Marshmallow rainbows. Ooo eee wala wala bing bang. Wham bam, thank you ma'am. 'Twas brillig, and the slithy toves did gyre and gimble in the wabe. I am the Walrus. Goo goo goo joob. The quick brown fox jumped over the lazy dogs. All work and no play makes Jack a dull boy. Sorry about that, Chief. There's no need to fear, Underdog is here. Yippee ky yi yea. Top of the morning to you.

Stephen Icarus and his sister chase after the small man wearing a green suit, green bowler, green socks, green shoes, green boxer shorts, and green suspenders. It's good to touch the green, green grass of home. God didn't make those little green apples and it don't rain in Indianapolis in the summertime. Over the river and through the woods. Can't see the forest from the trees. Catch-as-catch-can. Burn the candle at both ends. Easy come, easy go. First come, first served. Cha boom cha boom. Johnny Johnny Johnny Johnny whoops Johnny whoops Johnny Johnny Johnny Johnny. And this little pig went wee wee wee wee all the way home. You bet your sweet bippy.

The leprechaun finds a hot-air balloon, unties the rope looped around a tree trunk, hops into the basket and takes off into the sky.

—He's getting away! yells Stephen Icarus.

—Always after me Lucky charms, taunts the Leprechaun.

The branch of a tree punctures the balloon with a *pop*! The hot air escapes from the balloon like hot air escaping from a balloon sending the hot-air balloon careening back and forth across the sky like a hot-air balloon careening back and forth across the sky as it plummets back to earth.

—Yaieeeeeeeeeeee! the Leprechaun screams. Aieee! Aieeeee! Aieeeeeeeee!

The elf clad in green is caught by the branches of a tree.

The box of cereal tumbles back to earth and into the outstretched hands of Stephen Icarus whose ecstasy surpasses the orgiastic glee of catching a baseball hit into the grandstands during the World Series. Bingo bango bongo. Banzai!

—Always after me Lucky Charms.

The Leprechaun chortles from among the green leaves, abandoned like Prometheus.

—They're magically delicious!

It's Not Nice to Fool Mother Nature

In the style of Edgar Allan Poe

I must have been delirious—that is the only possible explanation I can muster. I do not expect anyone to believe my story—I scarcely believe it myself. Belief necessitates Faith, I have concluded; Faith is reliant upon Trust, but being that no logical proof or satisfactory evidence—other than my precarious testimony—can be summoned forth to adequately verify the bizarre incident I am about to confide, I expect my tale to be greeted with Doubt—as Fate has likely decreed.

I had been spending the night as a guest in a foreboding Gothic mansion, and in the middle of the night I awoke from an agitated slumber with an irrepressible urge for something to eat. While I had a gloomy premonition that all was not right in this bleak domain, I ventured through the many dark and somber passageways and downstairs to the kitchen without the slightest trepidation that I was about to witness an event of rueful horror. I say rueful—meaning full of rue—although abject or woeful or unparalleled might be more descriptive, but I have always fancied the sound of rueful and it seems most apropos.

I have said that I was plagued with hunger, and acting upon this bodily craving, I found a slice of bread, a knife from a cupboard drawer, and a plastic tub filled with yellow margarine. I placed all three items on the kitchen counter, opened the canister, used the knife to butter the bread, put the cover back on the tub, and took a bite from the bread. To my delight, the margarine did not taste like margarine at all. "It's butter," said I, earnestly convinced that the plastic tub had been filled with freshly churned butter.

No sooner had I said this, than I was answered by a voice from within the tub!—by a clear and deep and firm voice that might have risen from hell from the throat of a demon. "Parkay," it said.

I dared not speak! Could it be? Could a small plastic tub have spoken? I stood aghast in the solemn kitchen in that foreboding mansion, staring down at the tub, overcome by a sudden dizziness, paralyzed from fear. "Butter," I courageously insisted.

"Parkay," repeated the voice from within the tub, reverberating with authority.

I swooned back against the opposite wall, filled with terror, dropping the piece of bread in my hand. It fell, butter-side down, on the floor. My soul was suffused with rage—I was possessed to destroy this ghastly thing. I grew furious as I gazed upon the hideous tub of margarine. I rushed forward, grabbed the knife from the table, and buried it deep into the tub. But my blow was answered by a wailing shriek that curdled my blood. "Parkayyyyyy!" cried the tub in an agonized howl, writhing in pain. "Parkayyyyyy, Parkayyyy!" it groaned in muffled screams of anguish. Praying to Heaven above to save me from this gruesome beast, I thrust the knife into the tub again and again, until the awful thing spoke no more.

Did I not tell you that you would not believe my loathsome tale? Perhaps you simply think me mad, as well you should, for now—Almighty God! please no!—I still hear that voice, echoing through my head— *Butter! Parkay! Butter! Parkay!*—but I remain wholly convinced that I was morally justified in silencing that wretched tub of margarine—not simply because I could no longer bear that torturous voice of defiance, but because—it's not nice to fool Mother Nature.

Tony Tiger

In the style of William Blake

Tony Tiger, goodness sakes,
Eats a bowl of Frosted Flakes;
What brave artist dared create
The mighty beast who roars "They're G-R-R-REAT!"

In what circus, in what zoo,
Did the muses rendezvous?
Who drew a bib around your neck?
Who does your voice? A Slav? A Czech?

And what brave soul had the nerve,
To name you Tony instead of Irv?
What tiger likes Frosted Flakes,
Better than red juicy steaks?

SELLING OUT

When the artist laid down his quill,
Did your image give him a chill?
Was he fired? Forced to stop?
Or did he then draw Snap, Crackle, and Pop?

Tony Tiger, goodness sakes,
Eats a bowl of Frosted Flakes;
What brave artist dared create
The mighty beast who roars "They're G-R-R-REAT!"

Mmmm, Mmmm, Good

In the style of Upton Sinclair

Brick-red towers rose from Campbell's Soup Company. Billows of smoke bellowed forth, coloring the sky with a thick muddy hue. The rusty chemicals pouring from the majestic brick pillars had their origin in the large vats and kettles and steam rooms inside the colossal plant. Below the clouds of coarse soot, an arm of the Delaware river bubbled harshly; dark sewage oozed discrepantly from the factory, creating a vile bed of contorting, seething animal fat.

On the floor of the soup plant, Jurgis Rudkus forced a huge lever into place, sending a stream of broth gurgling through corroded steel pipes. The brown, bubbling mixture threw off strange and acrid fumes as it filled a huge vat. Jurgis had spent the better part of the morning trying to convince his fellow workers that he had seen a rodent race behind a huge boiler, slide over the lid's greasy surface, and plunge into the boiling caldron.

His co-workers simply laughed. Jurgis was forever telling tales of gloomy storage rooms where rats festered over piles of meat in disturbing numbers. Poisoned bread was frequently left out for the rats, and Jurgis reported that dead rat carcasses, poisoned bread, rancid meat scraps, and rat dung were often shoveled into the vats.

In truth, things were hurled into the soup vats that made the rats seem kosher. There were waterlogged planks of decaying wood infested with silverfish. There were old discarded machine parts coated with thick skins of rust. There were diseased cattle carcasses that had been left out to collect flies. Even if these things were to be fished out, little would be left recognizable after simmering in the broth all night.

The soup company could, through modern chemistry, give a slab of spoiled meat any color, flavor, or odor they wished, putting to use tripe, fat, trimmings, cartilage. Any scrap of meat could be ground up and treated with special chemicals to taste like anything the soup makers desired: Chicken Gumbo, Beef Boullion, Cream of Mushroom, Chicken and Stars. And whenever meat was so spoiled that it could not be used for anything else, it would be put into mighty grinders, mixed with other stale meats, and blended into broth. Mouldy meats and spoiled poultry that would otherwise have to be thrown out could now be treated scientifically with borax, glycerine, and food coloring.

His co-workers were amused by the detailed account, but when Jurgis climbed to the top of a stepladder and urged them to take action, they stared at him in disbelief. "Someone has to put a stop to this!" flared the Lithuanian immigrant, listing what he thought to be legitimate complaints against the managers of the soup plant. He claimed that working conditions were respon-sible for the afflictions suffered by his co-workers—that workers cooking Cheese Soup had orange-yellow skin from the food coloring, that the workers sorting letters to go in the Alphabet Soup were losing their vision, that workers making Cream of Broccoli had lost their ability to discern dairy products from vegetables.

His fellow workers merely laughed and walked away. Irate, Jurgis raised his clenched fist in the air and yelled after them at the exact moment the lunch whistle sounded. Startled, Jurgis stumbled back and flew from the ladder, knocking his head. There was a sudden, fierce splash, followed by a thick shower of broth.

After the lunch break, the floor manager, unable to find Jurgis, yelled out, "Now, where is that foreign ingrate?" None of his employees seemed to know, so he reached for a large lever, forcing the massive handle into place, sending a stream of broth pouring through corroded pipes toward a conveyer belt of oncoming tin cans. "Mmmmm, mmmmm, good," said the floor manager, unaware that he had just canned the world's first can of Cream of Jurgis.

Raid Kills Bugs Dead

In the style of Franz Kafka

Gregor Samsa shuffled the deck of cards and began to deal them to the three other vermin sitting around the table in the squalid hotel room. His numerous thin legs fluttered next to him as he slowly handed out the playing cards. Using his antennae, Gregor arranged his cards between two of his sticky little legs. He had dealt himself a royal flush, and while Gregor needed to maintain a poker face, he feared that the brownish liquid oozing from his mouth might give him away.

"Gaaa!" he exclaimed as he moved a pile of poker chips to the middle of the table with one of his squirming legs. He looked back at his cards. He sat nervously at the table, overcome with terror, hoping his appearance would not startle his fellow players, until he remembered these gangsters had also woken up one morning to find themselves changed into monstrous vermin. Gregor hated associating with these sinister insects, but when he was thrown out of his home by his father and his mother and his sister, he had been forced to turn to a life of crime.

"All right, boys, who's in?" asked Bugsy. The others moved their chips into the ante with their flailing long legs.

Suddenly there was a knock on the door. "Open up!" came a stern voice. "This is a raid!"

"A raid?!?" yelled Gregor. The others grabbed their guns from their leather holsters. Gregor slid from the chair and scampered under the bed.

The door burst open and Gregor could see a towering aerosol can of Raid insecticide standing in the open doorway.

"Raid!!!" yelled the other insects, backing against the walls. Suddenly the room filled with a thick fog of insecticide. From under the bed Gregor heard the other vermin coughing and gagging violently. Then came loud thuds as their bodies fell to the floor flat on their armored backs, their legs twitching madly through the fog, their small heads shaking frantically. Good God, thought Gregor, afraid to emerge from his hiding place.

Abruptly Gregor felt a sharp pain in his chest, his breathing was muffled, he felt searing cramps inside his vaulted brown belly, his sticky legs began to convulse uncontrollably, paralysis gripped his antennae. Desperate for air, Gregor wriggled out from under the bed and crawled up the wall toward the ceiling, but the whole room was beginning to spin, and Gregor fell back down on the table, knocking it over. He lay prostrate on the floor like his cronies, intoxicated by the fog, a startling, maddening pain burning through his head, his vision dimming. Gregor descended into a comalike sleep, and at last everything was quiet.

Reese's Peanut Butter Cup

In the style of William Faulkner

"You want to eat that chocolate." Caddy said. "You can eat it." She took the chocolate bar and unwrapped it and put it in my hand. The horses was stomping inside the barn. "Go ahead and eat the chocolate." Caddy said. "I know you want to eat it, Benjy."

The chocolate was brown like Reese's skin but it smelled sweeter than Reese's skin. Something was happening inside me and my head was spinning around and around and I was laughing and the bright shapes was going around too. I took a bite and it was on my chin and on my cheeks and it was tingly inside me and I began to cry and laugh at the same time.

Caddy was smiling. "I knew you wanted to eat that chocolate." Caddy said. "You eat it all." She smiled some more. Caddy smelled like hay. She smelled like fish too.

I was laughing and crying and I stood up and turned around to the follow the shapes of light on the grass. My shadow was long past the barn and I chased after it to catch up with the shadow of my head. "Wait." Caddy said. "Why are you running away from Caddy?"

I was turning around fast and I was thinking about the chocolate and how good it tasted and the bright shapes was going again and I went around the barn and all of a sudden I felt a big thump against my head and I fell down on the ground and I heard someone say Whooey and I couldn't stop.

Look what you did, Reese said. He made me look at what he was holding. It was a jar of peanut butter. A big piece of my chocolate bar was stuck in it. The piece of chocolate in my hand was covered with peanut butter. Stop that moaning and slobbering, Reese said. Benjy, if you dont stop making that racket, Im gonna whip you good. You better hush. You aint got nothing to moan about. So you've got peanut butter on your chocolate. That aint nothing to cry about. Im the one whos got chocolate in my peanut butter. Hush up, now, loony.

"What kind of boy would be behind the barn eating peanut butter from a jar with a spoon?" Addie Bundren asked.

"A hungry boy." Vardaman said. I hope he dont get too hungry though, thought Vardaman. My father's a fish.

"I'll shoot the scoundrel." Addie Bundren said. "Everyone in Jefferson knows he was up to no good. All of Yoknapatawpha County suspects something went on behind the barn up yonder."

"What went on behind the barn?" Vardaman asked.

"What barn?" Addie said.

I could hear Caddy coming after me. What in tarnation happened? Caddy asked.

He ran plum right into me, Miss Caddy, said Reese. His chocolate bar broke off into my jar of peanut butter.

Reese took the broken piece of chocolate out of his peanut butter and looked it over. This may not be such a bad thing at all, Reese said. I reckon this might just be the start of something good. This tastes mighty fine. Hush your bellering, loony, and take a bite of your chocolate bar together with the peanut butter. This is tasty all right. Two great tastes in one. I bet some rich white folks would buy this for a quarter so I can go to the show tonight. You aint got no extra quarter, does you, Miss Caddy, for a piece of chocolate with some peanut butter on it?

I took a bite of the chocolate and my head started swirling with the bright shapes. They was going round and round. Caddy told me to sit down by the side of the barn and eat my chocolate.

Caddy handed Reese a quarter. "Take off them pants of yours, Reese." Caddy said.

"Begging your pardon, Miss Caddy?"

"You just take off them pants." Caddy said.

The barn was dark. Caddy was on her knees. She found another chocolate bar that Reese must have been hiding and she put some of the peanut butter on it with her fingers. She made sure there was peanut butter all over the chocolate bar. Caddy started to lick the peanut butter off the chocolate bar with her tongue. Then I could see inside the barn and I started to cry. Whooey, hollered Reese. Sure do beat sassprilluh, said Caddy. Whooey. The horses whinnied.

I couldn't stop crying. "Hush, Benjy." Caddy said. She knelt down and put her arms around me. She held me tight. "You aint going to say nothing, are you, Benjy?" Caddy asked. "Course not." Caddy laughed. "You cant talk none." I still couldn't quit crying. "Hush now." Caddy said. "I like your discovery, Benjy. Chocolate and peanut butter together. I aint going to let no one say you is a loony no more. Youre the genius of Yoknapatawpha County. You is, Benjy."

Reese smelled like peanut butter. Caddy smelled like not so sweet chocolate.

The Good News Razor

In the style of Sylvia Plath

I hate you, King Gillette.
You're not royalty.
You tricked me—
With your disposable razors,
you Nazi bastard.

What is the damn Good News
If your double safety blade,
Sealed in cruddy blue plastic,
Can't get a close shave
Let alone slit my wrist?

SELLING OUT

If it's Good News you want—
I will castrate you, Herr Gillette.
With your cheap blue plastic
Nazi war toy.

Grey Poupon Mustard

In the style of Tom Wolfe

Sherman McCoy sat in the back of a terrific black Rolls-Royce limousine, his long nose riding parallel to the horizon, like the needle of a compass clad in a *zip zip zip zip yaggghhhh* double-breasted white silk suit custom-tailored in Hong Kong before he took the hydrofoil to Macau, $300 patent-leather wing-tip shoes bought in Florence after a delightful morning spent admiring Botticellis and Brunelleschis at the Uffizi, and a peppermint-striped button-down shirt accented by a yellow *dot dot dot dot dot dot* silk tie and matching silk handkerchief *ka-ching ka-ching*! His chauffeur, a man named James, the required appellation among chauffeurs for the Anglo-Protestant Yale-educated Park Avenue Wall Street flotilla, was driving the sumptuous car confidently along an empty road in rural Westchester. The street was surrounded by lush green slopes . . . heavy oak trees . . . leaves turning yellow and orange and red . . . the limousine glided slowly . . . a cagey blazing Dunn and Bradstreet Chase Manhattan uneasiness crept into Sherman's blowdried skull . . . There was a second limousine approaching his . . . it moved slowly . . . advanced tentatively . . . an odd coincidence . . . identical limousines on a solitary country road . . . two ships passing at noon . . . the two limousines stopped alongside one another . . . the electric black-tinted window of the approaching limousine slowly glided open . . . obviously an admirer. Sherman pressed a silver-plated switch with his forefinger. As his window lowered, he could hear the soft *whirr whirr whirr whirr whirr whirr.*

A dignified elderly balding man wearing a tuxedo was sitting in the back of the other limousine. "Pardon me, do you have any Grey Poupon mustard?" he asked.

It was a cultured genteel aristocratic voice. *Some kind of scam artist! Next he'll be asking me for my wallet! He* looks harmless enough. *Why doesn't he have his own mustard? What kind of idiot would be driving around without a jar of Grey Poupon mustard in his limousine?* He's obviously a man of rich tastes. *What's wrong with you? The man's begging for mustard! He's going to rob you blind.*

What harm could come from lending a helping hand? *For all you know he's a serial killer. He asks for mustard then he takes your life!* Sherman reached for his jar of Grey Poupon mustard and handed it out the window to the stranger.

The stranger took the jar of mustard, nodded in appreciation, and rolled up his window. *Whirrrrr.*

"Hey, wait a minute," said Sherman. But it was too late. The chauffeur of the other limousine stepped on the gas . . . *varoom zoom zoom zoom* . . . the duplicate black limousine rocketed down the street . . . *screech screech screech* . . . pushing the envelope . . . BAAAAVOOOOOMMMMM . . . breaking the sound barrier . . . and it was gone as mysteriously as it had first appeared.

"I knew it," said Sherman McCoy, sitting up straight in the plush leather seat of his limousine. "James, get my insurance company on the car phone. We've been robbed." He pushed the silver-plated button again with his forefinger and the window whirred shut tight again.

Only Her Hairdresser Knows for Sure

In the style of Agatha Christie

My old friend Hercule Poirot, the Belgian ex-detective, nodded his egg-shaped head, twisted the end of his waxed military moustache, and took another sip of his blackcurrant.

"The dead man's only offense was choosing hair-dressing as a profession," said Poirot, straightening the decanter on the table next to his leather chair.

"I don't understand, Poirot. A pair of hair scissors were found in the hairdresser's back. What about the gloves found by Chief Inspector Japp? Are you forgetting the cigarette ash and the fingerprints? Aren't you overlooking the broken wristwatch with its hands stopped at exactly three o'clock, fifteen minutes before the murder actually took place?"

"Once again, Hastings, you underestimate the methods of the indomitable Hercule Poirot. I do not run to and fro looking for clues. It is just as easy to lie back in one's chair, mull over all the evidence, sift some *sirop de cassis*, drift off into an occasional cat nap, gently ridicule my protégé, and come up with the answer. My work is done from within *here*—" Poirot tapped his egg-shaped head with grandiloquent self-satisfaction. "I trust the little grey cells, *mon ami!*"

As usual, this pompous altercation incited my rancor. "Dash it all! If that is so, Poirot, why didn't you anticipate that the hairdresser would be murdered immediately after he sent you a letter requesting your help? Has it not occurred to you that anyone who entreats your aid when you are investigating a case is murdered just moments before you arrive on the scene? Engaging your assistance is a death knell."

"Touché, my dear Hastings," said the Belgian, swigging down the rest of his blackcurrant and then leaning back with an amused grin. "One murder always leads to another. In trying to cover up their tracks, criminals invariably betray themselves. When Madame Christine Cavendish hired me to investigate the murder of her husband, retired Colonel Reginald Cavendish, discovered with a knife in his back in the library at Satterthwaite Manor, I suspected the identity of the murderer immediately after Chief Inspector Japp and his men from Scotland Yard found Cavendish's daughter, Emily, strangled to death and stuffed into the manor's grandfather clock. My suspicions were further aroused when Major Riddle found a revolver, a suicide note scrawled in blue ink, and the Cavendish family dog—a Labrador retriever named Nigel—shot in the head and packed into a steamer trunk checked into Left Luggage at Charring Cross Station. My hunch was almost certainly confirmed when the body of my secretary Miss Lemon was found floating in the Thames. But with the murder of this hairdresser, Reginald Cavendish's killer has positively given herself away."

"But why would anyone kill a hairdresser?"

"Precisely. That is the question I have asked myself over and over. Why would anyone kill a hairdresser?" Poirot shook his head and repeated the question to himself. "Why would anyone kill a hairdresser? Why would anyone kill a hairdresser?"

"Maybe someone wasn't pleased with her haircut," I offered.

"At last, you are using the little grey cells, *mon ami*," said Poirot, tapping his finger to his head with the superciliousl conceit I have come to relish. "But your reasoning is like that of a schoolboy. The facts, considered methodically, permit only one explanation. At first I considered Colonel Mustard in the library with the lead pipe, but that proved unsatisfactory. Then there was the matter of the strawberries, but that failed to take into account the fact that there was a secret in Madame Cavendish's life—there can be no doubt of that. Her hairdresser was killed for knowing that secret."

"Are you suggesting the hairdresser was blackmailing her?" I queried.

"You are completely off the track, Hastings. Colonel Cavendish was murdered by his wife. It was Madame Cavendish who stood to inherit his fortune."

"But the butler and all the servants said they saw a woman with grey hair leaving the scene of the crime. Madame Cavendish is a brunette."

"With Clairol hair coloring, it is virtually impossible to tell whether a woman with grey hair dyes it brown," said Poirot, tapping his finger to his egg-shaped head.

"Does she? Or doesn't she?" I asked.

"Only her hairdresser knows for sure," replied Poirot. "That's why Madame Cavendish killed him. He was about to reveal her secret to me, but before he could do so, he was sent to that great beauty salon in the sky."

He paused, taking a sip of his blackcurrant, and silently we both reflected on how tragically a petty secret had cost an innocent hairdresser his life.

Maytag's Complaint

In the style of Philip Roth

Having the loneliest job in the world gives me plenty of time to do what I do best, namely jerkin' the gherkin, whacking the ham, pulverizing the salami, *shtupping* the *shvantz*, honing the bone, yanking the yahoo, incessantly afraid that the shocked owner of a Maytag washer is going to walk in on me to find my pants around my ankles, my piston-like fist pumping furiously, just as I squirt a wad of that strange combination of liquid fabric softener and Brylcream into an old sock, a coffee mug, a hat, an empty box of Milk Duds, or one of the washing machines here in the shop. I often imagine a voluptuous buxom woman who looks exactly like Naomi Steinberg, the girl back in high school with the biggest pair of headlights I ever saw in my life, entering my shop on the pretext of wanting to have her washer repaired, but who, upon seeing me pulling my pud, doffs her skintight turtleneck, unhooks her brassiere, and holds up her soft fleshy melons for me so I can eat to the beat as they bounce to and fro, but suddenly I remember that Maytag washers are built so well they never need repair, so not only will I be deprived a hot, salivating tryst with a top-heavy nymphomaniac on top of a Maytag washer, but the only way I'll be putting any tools to use between nine and five is by porking my palm with my circumcised cucumber.

Doctor, why do I, Alexander Maytag, love this lonely job? No, the name was originally Maytagowitz, changed at Ellis Island when my grandfather arrived from some *shtetl* in Eastern Europe where they cleaned their *shmattas* with a washboard and a tub, and they were grateful for the *ferchadat* washboard and tub! That's my mother talking! I suddenly remember how my *meshuggeneh* mother, Sophie Maytag, inflicted me with guilt because my clothes were cleaned in a machine! You should be grateful for that washing machine! In the old country, they washed what little clothes they had in the river! You should thank God almighty that you don't have to *schlepp* your dirty laundry down the Hudson River and beat them on a rock! Maybe that's it, Doctor! Maybe that's why I'm still hopelessly beating my kosher pink pickle! Pulling my putz is self-flagellation to compensate for the 3,000 years the Jewish people spent washing their clothes in rivers! Yes, that's why I locked myself in the bathroom to wax my wang on the day of my Bar Mitzvah, why as an adolescent I spilled my vile ooze into a lady's purse in a changing room in Gimbel's, why on a date with *zaftig* Sylvia Feinstein I pumped my custard into an empty popcorn box in Radio City Music Hall, why just last week I shot my gissum into an airsick bag at 35,000 feet, why I jostle my John Thomas fifteen, sixteen, maybe seventeen times a day at work—inciting the wrath of the American Rabbinical Association, the Anti-Defamation League, the United Jewish Appeal, the Simon Wiesenthal Center, Hadassah, and the "girls" in my mother's Mah Jongg circle for jeopardizing the sovereignty of Israel should I be caught red-handed.

Is that it, doctor? Is my perverse, degrading self-abuse simply a rebellion against two sets of dishes, the *meshugge* laws that forbid us from drinking a glass of milk with a bologna sandwich, and that accusing, castigating, guilt-inflicting, humiliating, castrating *momzer* of a mother, Sophie Maytag, who washed my clothes in a machine rather than using a washboard and a tub until her fingers bled? Am I really that big a *shmuck*? Tell me, Doctor, is that why I chose the loneliest job on earth?